Havana

The Photography of
Hans Engels

HAVANA

The Photography of Hans Engels

With an Introduction
by Beth Dunlop

and a Contribution
by María Elena Martín Zequeira

Prestel

Munich · London · New York

For Teresa

The photographer wishes to express his special thanks to:
Anita Hernandez, journalist, for helping bring this project to its feet;
María Elena Martín Zequeira, architect, for her knowledge of Havana;
Heike and Jörg von Schleebrügge for their selfless dedication;
Dr. Traugott Schöfthaler of the German UNESCO Commission
for his interest in the project;
and Cubana and Kodak for their generous support.

Cover
Cuban Telephone Company in Centro Habana
Architects: Morales and Co., 1927
Frontispiece
López Serrano apartment building
Architects: Mira and Rosich, 1931
Back cover
Cinema Riviera
Architect: José Luaces, 1957
Manuel López Chaves residence
Architect: Esteban Rodríguez Castells, 1932
Palacio de las Ursulinas (far left) and adjacent structures
Architect: José Toraya, 1913

Library of Congress Catalog Card Number: 99-62960

© Prestel Verlag, Munich · London · New York, 1999
© all photographs by Hans Engels

Prestel Verlag
Mandlstrasse 26, D-80802 Munich, Germany
Tel. +49 (89) 38 17 09-0, Fax +49 (89) 38 17 09-35
4 Bloomsbury Place, WC1A 2QA London, England
Tel. +44 (171) 323-5004, Fax +44 (171) 636-8004
and 16 West 22nd Street, New York, NY 10010, USA
Tel. (212) 627-8199, Fax (212) 627-9866

Prestel books are available worldwide.
Please contact your nearest bookseller or write to any
of the above addresses for information concerning
your local distributor.

Copyedited by Judith Gilbert
Designed by Rainald Schwarz, Munich
Lithography by Fotolito Longo, Bolzano
Printed by Jütte Druck, Leipzig
Bound by Kunst- und Verlagsbuchbinderei, Baalsdorf

Printed in Germany on acid-free paper

ISBN 3-7913-2157-9

Contents

Havana
The Photography of Hans Engels

By Beth Dunlop

In the pages that follow, you will not see a book that is merely about a place, nor photographs that are merely about photography. Hans Engels' study of the buildings of twentieth-century Havana is far more complex and penetrating than that. Indeed, this is a book that deals with a powerful abstract concept: the way in which time affects space. It is a concept that might confound a physicist, much less a photographer. The physicist has the rules of science to help probe the mysteries of this; the photographer has just a camera and film, and of course the subject matter, but it takes more than just technical expertise to infuse two-dimensional objects with a presence that is more than just images on paper. The buildings and streetscapes that Hans Engels depicts here speak to us of yesterday, today, and tomorrow. They are resonant with history, and with culture, and they tell us a story that is not really about architecture at all, but one of change and immutability, of despair and hope.

The subject at hand is Havana, but not the Havana necessarily of today. In this book, you will not find photographs that bespeak a specific day or year or even decade; rather you will see photographs that are ageless because they are as much about time as place. And yet—I realize that this is a powerful conundrum— these photographs impart more about a place, this particular place, Havana, than many others, precisely because they are not fixed in a particular moment. They are indeed buildings that are the witness to four decades of Fidel Castro's rule in Cuba, years of turmoil and impoverishment, years in which mere survival domi-nated other concerns, among them the preservation of buildings. Of the pho-tographs in this book, only one (an apartment building by Antonio Quintana) was constructed after Castro came to power, and standing alone out of the context of its street or neighborhood in brutalist isolation, it reflects the harshness that domi-nated both the country and the architecture of the time. It provides a counterpoint to all else in the book, buildings that stand with enormous grace and distinction, some of them lofty and some much more mundane—all, however, imbued with a kind of nobility and with passion.

Havana has always been a city of elemental, even overpowering, beauty, a city of enormous presence on an island of magnificent geology, topography, and land-scape. The first recorded descriptions of Cuba come to us from Christopher Colum-bus' initial trip in 1492 when, sitting offshore in the vessel *Santa Maria* he wrote, "I have never seen such a beautiful place." On that first voyage, Columbus spent five weeks in Cuba and returned the following year to explore it once again. What he found was a long and narrow island, the largest tropical archipelago in the West, with fertile plains, a wealth of rivers, and five different mountain ranges. The north-ernmost coast of the island, the land that would ultimately become Havana and its environs, had emerged from the ice ages with a steep and eroded coastline, with outcroppings of limestone and tiny fine sandy beaches.

Cinema Arenal. 41st St. between 30th and 34th Sts., Playa, Havana

The earliest island inhabitants lived in caves or in primitive hand-built shelters; archaeologists have found evidence of inhabitation dating back to 3500 B.C., as cave discoveries and excavations on open land have yielded pictographs, tools, pot shards, and other artifacts of early civilization. By the time Columbus arrived in Cuba, the tribes were a mix of Ciboney and Arawak (also known as Taino) Indians, and the fiercely warlike Caribs, recent arrivals from South America.

By 1511, however, the balance had begun to shift as settlers from the neighboring island of Hispaniola began the process of the European settlement of Cuba. By 1516, there were seven permanent settlements established on the island, including one that Columbus himself called El Puerto de Carenas but was then, in turn, named Batabano, then San Cristobal de la Habana, and ultimately just Habana (or Havana). The actual site of Havana was itself moved in stages to the western part of the bay, as a great awareness developed of the strategic necessities of defending both the new settlement and the island from the steady siege of pirates and others. By 1519, the city was established, and the first mass was held in the Plaza de Armas as the official christening of the town. Even then, Havana—and Cuba—were indeed as they were often described, "the jewel of the Spanish crown." Historians relate that Spanish soldiers regarded an assignment to St. Augustine, Florida (a place of considerable beauty and allure itself) as punishment; Havana was the prize.

Havana, then, was ruled by the water; it was its harbor that made it most significant. The Cuban-born Miami architect Andres Duany points out that Havana was the great crossroads of the Caribbean, the first stop on arrival from Europe and the last before departure; he terms it a city shaped by gold and calls it the "Rome of the Caribbean," in that all sea routes led there. Indeed it was "landfall" for the Spanish galleons carrying treasure, the safe harbor from storms at sea and from the ever-present threat of pirates seeking plunder. As the gold and pre-Columbian treasures passed through the harbor, some of it, inevitably, remained, and Havana became a very rich city and stayed that way as the economy changed from one based on gold and booty to one based on sugar and tobacco.

It was also a fortified city, a city of "castillos" and "fortaleza." Yet as the decades passed, Havana developed under the many influences that led to the architecture which we now think of as being particular to the Spanish New World—buildings that spring from Moorish-Spanish and Greco-Roman influences, but built within the limits of materials and skills of the craftsmen who lived in the newly developing city. Havana was planned initially behind fortified walls according to a strict colonial hierarchy and with the gridded urban layout prescribed by the Law of the Indies.

"As the city of Havana evolved at the end of the sixteenth century, so did the urban grid," wrote the Italian photojournalist Nicolas Sapieha. "A chess board, its pieces were the buidings that defined the squares, and the emerging city blocks, configured by narrow rectangular streets." The earliest buildings relied on available materials, reflecting the Mudejar traditions of Moorish Spain and using, as Duany says, "the traditional materials of the earth." Spanish influence remains today in the tilework, stone, painted ceilings, and stained glass. The ever-evolving architecture of Havana took European styles—the Baroque, Neoclassical, Beaux Arts, and the emerging modern movements, beginning with Art Nouveau and Art Deco—and transformed them, sometimes slightly and sometimes greatly, to add up to a body of work that is remarkable in its extent and intensity.

Still, the history of architecture in Havana is a history of both individual buildings and of a profound sense of urbanism. Ernest Hemingway wrote of a city "looking fine in the sun." The writer Alejo Carpentier described Havana as a city of columns, and indeed, that is the case. It is also a city of broad landscaped boulevards, the products of the grand urban plans of recent centuries. The landscapes of the last decades are often impromptu ones, wild gardens that have arrived to take over where the architecture no longer fills the land, as if nature was reclaiming its percentage.

Scholarship on the history of architecture in Cuba is relatively sparse when measured against that of other countries of comparable size and historical importance, and much of what has been written remains untranslated from the original

Row houses on Malecón and San Nicolás, Centro Habana

Spanish. Even so, the ground is fertile for debate. Is the work in Havana comparatively primitive due to its mixing of styles and limitations of craftmanship, as Rachel Carley asserts? Is it too frequently viewed through the eyes of those who impose European standards of style and history on it with little comprehension of its cultural complexity, as Jorge Rigau would suggest? Or is it, as Paul Goldberger points out, "one of the richest and most eclectic urban environments anywhere, overflowing with architecture that is extravagant in its ambition and spectacular in its execution"?

Duany, who has made several trips to Havana to study both architecture and urban form, and who has written on the subject (in Spanish), states definitively: "What is extraordinary about Cuba and its architecture is that, of the many types to be found there, it is all first rate. No matter by what miracle or what means this happened, it should not be discounted."

With more than 900 buildings of architectural note, Old Havana has since become a UNESCO World Heritage Site and has attracted both domestic and, with the easing of travel restrictions to Cuba, international recognition. The remainder of Havana is receiving less institutional attention, at least in terms of preserving its architecture. The architect and historian Eduardo Luis Rodriguez has become an impassioned proponent of preserving not just the architecture of each era but of the urban form of Havana. Duany, along with several other architects and designers (most of whom are of Cuban descent), has begun to study that form to create a code to allow the city to grow and rebuild without endangering what is there now, including the scale and shape of the city.

For those who have seen it, Havana remains a great revelation. Duany talks of his first reaction to buildings he recalls from his boyhood as being "almost physiological, like an electrical shock, a thrilling feeling."

El Centro de Oro Building. Reina and Campanario, Centro Habana. Architect: Eugenio Dediot, ca. 1910

That visceral response is one which in many ways can only be experienced in person. To this day, most of the world has not been so lucky. That is why Hans Engels' photographs are a powerful document and more. Through his camera lens we are able to witness the wonder of Havana's architecture.

Engels is a photographer not merely by profession but by calling. He picked up his first camera, one that belonged to a friend, at age twelve, and there was no turning back; from his first contact with a camera, he wanted to be a photographer. The camera, as he recalls it, was a Pentax, and, he said, "I took photos of everything that is of interest to a young boy. I am sure I had no concept of what I was doing at that time, and I think a friend's sister was the first subject I photographed." Engels went on to study at the Bayerische Staatslehranstalt für Photographie (School of Photography of the Bavarian State) and was then hired as the assistant to a commercial photographer. He stayed a single day, realizing immediately that he needed to do his own work, not someone else's. From there, he set up a studio as a still-life photographer and worked as a photojournalist.

In 1986, Engels was awarded the Danner scholarship for photography and as a result traveled through Europe for a year to work on a project entitled "Zeit-Räume" (a term that does not have a good counterpart in English; a literal translation would be "Time—Rooms"). The scholarship took him to Italy, France, Germany, Austria, Switzerland, and also Poland, after the fall of the Iron Curtain. "In Poland I saw for the first time the influence of the political system and poverty on the people and on the buildings. Living conditions there were miserable, but for my work it was very inspiring," the photographer later said.

Engels photographed turn-of-the-century palaces—hotels, casinos, and spas— long forgotten and beginning to decay. "The atmosphere of these places inspired me," he recalled. "Up to that date architecture hadn't been of much importance to me. What interested me was rather to see how a building changes through time." With camera in hand he began to investigate the many factors, physical and social, that cause buildings to transform over the years, ranging from the deleterious effect of climate on structure to the impact of inhabitation by the homeless.

From those explorations came his first two published works, a book about castles in former communist East Prussia and one on "Zeiträume," which was accompanied by an exhibition of the same name at the Stadtmuseum (city museum) in Munich, the Mois de la Photo in Paris, and in the Galerie Faber in Vienna.

As that work drew to a close, Engels started pondering the next step, thinking about where else in the world he might find similar conditions of poverty and neglect, of buildings left to deteriorate over time. Havana seemed a logical destination. He made two trips to Havana in 1997, during which he photographed only Art Deco buildings; a subsequent trip in 1999 led him to other twentieth-century structures. "On my first trip to Havana I was completely overpowered by the architecture, on the one hand, and by the people on the other. Diligence, poverty, improvisation, patience, humor, musicality, interest and a sense of business.... It seemed pure cynicism to take photographs of the aesthetic of the decay of Havana. On the contrary, I was surprised to see the vitality and variety of Havana's architecture and decided that it was worth documenting as a topic of its own."

That the photos in this book are entirely of twentieth-century buildings is note-worthy in itself, in that these—oddly—are often less cared for than those centuries older. Historians in Cuba and elsewhere have been working desperately to accord equal status to important endangered structures in the city regardless of age, which might be considered a qualitative rather than chronological approach to conservation. At first Engels tried to compile a thorough documentation, recording buildings from each era and of each style. But he abandoned that and let his own artistic muse rule instead: "The basis of my work was the inspiration I drew from seeing the place with my own eyes on my bicycle tours of the city. Of course I tried to show the best examples of the stylistic periods. But it never was my goal to give a complete documentation of Havana's architecture; it was more important for me to show the dignity and elegance of the buildings."

Like the structures he photographs, Engels uses a timeless approach to the artistic and technical aspects of his work. He uses a Sinar camera with a 4 x 5 inch format, standing (or crouching, or kneeling, depending on the angle) under a dark-ening cloth, just as photographers did a century ago.

He does not take many photographs and then choose among them; he takes just one, after using Polaroids to test his aesthetic, to feel and see the light. Most of these images were taken during the two separate months of February, 1997 and 1999; that was the month he found optimal for architectural photography.

In Havana, Engels rode up and down streets and through squares on a broken bicycle, "to let myself be inspired by the city." For the final photographs, with larger equipment, he traveled by cab, which meant more planning. "But I also like coinci-dences, and part of this documentation is spontaneous inspiration. The basic prin-ciple for my work is, 'Keep your eyes and mind open.' " In two months in Havana, he took 125 photos of which 78 appear in this book.

The photographs themselves tell a story on their own. There are, here, haunting images of buildings that seem to speak about more than just the men who made them or the materials they are made of. These photographs are eerily profound, images of ghosts of bygone eras that have become entrapped in time. Standing alone in somber isolation or fitted into an urban complex, the buildings that Engels depicts have both dignity and pathos. This is not a didactic study, not a book in which one can trace the evolution of nearly 500 years of Havana's history and judge the fairly perilous straits of its architecture; it is, instead, an individual look at a more subtle circumstance, which is to say architecture, and culture, of a single century.

To capture what has happened in a comparatively short time frame is to create a picture of poverty and neglect indeed. Paint is peeling off stucco; dirt and grime cover even quite recent structures. There are makeshift shutters and windows. What is lost has not been replaced; what remains is still in use or has found new function and context. And yet, Engels has found hope where others might see only hopelessness, and his photographs impart this. "Despite the decay, Havana is unique in the world because of the variety of architectural styles found there," he says. Poverty and not governmental conservation projects has preserved the build-ings. That is how this documentation came into being.

Apartment building. 107–113 Marina, Centro Habana. Architect: Victor M. Morales, 1951

The Havana Photographs

1 Previous page: Julio Alvarez Arcos residence
2/3 Mark Anthony Pollack residence

4 Guillermina Pérez residence
5 Cuban Telephone Company

6 Alberto de Armas residence

7 Multifamily house in Vedado

8 Housing estate in Miramar
9 Juan V. Aguilera residence

11 Villa in Víbora

12 Association of the Clerks of Commerce
13 Residences in Vedado
14 Emilio Iglesias residence

15 Private residence in Vedado
16 Cinema Cuba

17/18 Row houses on Malecón

19 Palacio de las Ursulinas (far left)

20 El Centro de Oro Building
21 Jose Miguel Gómez residence

23/24 Gran Teatro de la Habana

25 Doorway with Art Nouveau motifs
26 Apartment building in Habana Vieja

27 Quinta Rosario Secondary School
28 Palacio Cueto

29 Casa de Dámasco Gutiérrez Cano

30 Cinema Arenal
31 Apartment buildings in Centro Habana
32 Pilar Antonia Lluch residence

33 Herminia García Bruna residence

34/35 Bacardí Building
36 La Casa Quintana store

38 López Serrano apartment building

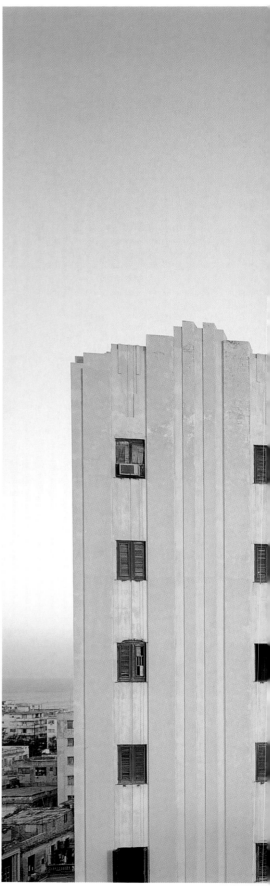

39/40/41 López Serrano Building

42 Apartment building in Centro Habana
43 Casa de las Américas

46 Apartment building in Centro Habana

47 El País Newspaper Building
48 Apartment buildings in Centro Habana

49 Apartment building in Vedado

50 City residence in Centro Habana

51 Residence in Vedado

52 Ricardo Hernández Beguerie residence

53 Entrance to the Maca apartment building

55/56 Emilio Vasconcelos residence

58 Apartment building in Playa

59 Olan Tower Building

61 Apartment building in Vedado
62 Cuban Tobacco Industry Building
63 Alfred de Schulthess residence

64 Synagogue
65 School of Dentistry

67 Residence in Miramar

68 Sephardic Hebrew Center of Cuba

69 Bartolomé Masó Secondary School

70 Apartment building in Centro Habana

71 Apartment building in Miramar

73 Modern "redesign" of an Eclectic building
74 Residential high-rise in Centro Habana

75 Row houses in Centro Habana

76 Solimar Building
77 Apartment building in Vedado

The Architecture of a Century

By María Elena Martín Zequeira, Architect

For natives it is difficult to talk about Havana without exaggerating. Although small, Havana is an exceptional Caribbean city not only in terms of its geography, people, and vintage cars, but specifically because of its architecture. The stylistic diversity of its buildings and the tradition of city planning, in which works of different periods coincide, make Havana comparable to much larger cities. That is Havana: simultaneously unsophisticated and affluent, discreet and gorgeous—a magic city for strolling, a city to be respected and loved. Although Havana Vieja is included on the World Heritage List because of its unquestionably historic value, its twentieth-century architecture is also of great significance in the urban fabric because of its tremendous quality and originality and impact on Havana's image as Cuba's capital. All cities reflect the lives of the people living in them; buildings speak volumes about traditions and trends, painting a portrait of civic endeavor. They "talk" to us about daily life at a particular historic moment. This book highlights a moment unfairly overlooked in Havana's architectural history: the transition from Art Deco in the 1930s to Modernism in the 1950s.

Havana, the hub of trade relations between the former Spanish empire and its colonies in the Americas, was founded in 1519. For almost four centuries it was under colonial rule, and its first buildings and neighborhoods were conceived by architects and engineers sent from Spain. In 1898, Cuba obtained its independence and a Republic was soon established in 1902, after a period of American military intervention. Once free from the Spanish crown, Cuba experienced great economic and social growth, especially in its capital. Its doors opened to other cultures, and its existing population of Spaniards, Africans, Indians, and Asians was further enriched by new waves of immigrants. All these changes had a remarkable influence on the shape of the city in the first decades of the twentieth century. The monumental image of Greater Havana consolidating in the 1920s and 1930s is heavily indebted to French landscape artist Jean-Claude-Nicolas Forestier, who worked in Cuba and abroad to put Havana in an outstanding position in the Caribbean. Besides Forestier, other well-known architects visited the city during the twentieth century. Some of them left their imprint through their teachings or projects for future development, others through their buildings—underscoring the importance of

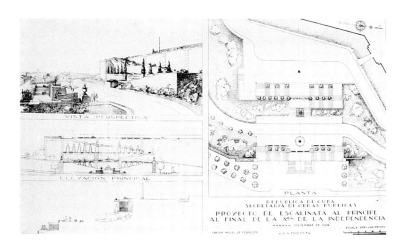

View of the Paseo del Prado, La Habana Vieja, before its last renovation in 1929 by J.C.N. Forestier and Raul Otero (above)
J.C.N. Forestier, project for Malecón between the Plaza del Maine and the Avenida de los Presidentes, El Vedado, 1928 (below)

Havana on the American continent. The first group includes Jose Luís Sert, Walter Gropius, Philip Johnson, and, more recently, Ricardo Bofill and Andres Duany; the second includes Thomas Hastings, Walker and Gillete, Schultze and Weaver,

"La Marina" Newspaper Building, La Habana Vieja; currently the Plaza Hotel, renovated in 1908 by José F. Mata

John H. Duncan, Torre de Reloj, Quinta Avenida, Miramar, 1920

Linea Street, El Vedado neighborhood, at the beginning of the twentieth century

McKim, Mead and White, Richard Neutra, Felix Candela, and Welton Becket and Associates. This coming and going of international personalities in the field of architecture and city planning, combined with the work of equally outstanding Cuban architects, make Havana a living museum.

But what sets Havana apart from other Latin American and world capitals? First, its scale. Although it has many tall buildings, much of Havana has always been human-scale, a place to be hand-touched and surrounded by porches and gardens which allow for an ongoing dialogue between the city and its residents. There are no superhighways, and streets are never wide enough to become a barrier between the sidewalks. Second, although the city grew under strict urban codes, architectural variety is one of its main characteristics since individual architects left their marks on buildings that stand out for their innovative design. Third, traditional Havanan architecture is interwoven with international models followed at a particular time. Nothing significant has been demolished, and even though certain buildings have been modified, remodeled, and tailored to fit new needs, original facades have been preserved, creating interesting juxtapositions between different stylistic periods. In fact, most structures dating from colonial times to the present still exist, although most of them demand urgent attention.

Still, in general, those who constructed the city did not pay equal attention to its public spaces, parks, squares, and gardens. Perhaps the constant presence of greenery in and around homes and along avenues and streets suggests that the people in Havana were not interested in creating public sites for rest and leisure. In general, city parks are small and inadequate. Up until now, the natural environment has not been included efficiently in the urban layout. The Almendares River, the most important river in town, does not have an important role, and the coastline has not been incorporated into urban life. Only the sea walk, the Malecón—about four miles long—has an active part in the daily life of Havana's population and is an attraction for the growing number of Cuba's tourists.

In the second half of the nineteenth century, the city began to overflow the walls which confined it; their demolition began in 1863, and today only a few standing sections of it indicate its original layout. New neighborhoods mushroomed along the roads connecting the old town to the countryside while new residential suburbs, a modern concept at the time, began to be built. Most significant among them were Las

Murallas, El Carmelo, and El Vedado. As its name clearly indicates, Las Murallas developed in the area where the original walls had been, which perhaps was the reason it became the new cultural and administrative center of town. In this neighborhood the tallest buildings—hotels, theaters, office buildings, markets, and cultural centers—began to rise along wide, straight avenues, contrasting with the narrow fabric of the old town. Because the area was also residential, it became famous for the fancy homes of the politicians and businessmen interspersed between those of the poor and middle class.

View of El Vedado neighborhood before the construction of its tallest buildings by the end of the 1950s

El Carmelo and El Vedado neighborhoods—adopted by Havana's city hall in 1859 and 1860 respectively, and which later expanded to the north, east, and south—were located along the coastline, the Almendares River, and current Zapata Street. Both were conceived as residential suburbs with facilities for education, trade, religion, and leisure, and were each characterized by gridded layouts composed of square blocks encircled by gardens and porches. Although conceived in the nineteenth century, they did not gain acceptance from wealthier Havana residents anxious to escape the crowded downtown until the first part of the twentieth century. Other neighborhoods such as Miramar, La Vibora, and Centro Habana continued to grow during the first decades of the twentieth century and therefore are characterized by a variety of Eclectic, Art Nouveau, Art Deco, and Modern architecture that coexists along their streets and avenues.

Eclecticism

Prior to the early part of the twentieth century, examples of Eclectic architectural trends already popular in Europe and the United States could be found in Havana, where they were also identified with progress and innovation. Thus, between 1900 and 1950, local architects developed countless examples of this style, which is marked by profuse ornamentation, overstated facades and interiors, and high-quality construction, as well as prominent staircases. Typically made of decorative materials such as marble, granite, stucco, rare woods, or cast metal, these stairwells were usually backed by one or more brightly colored, stained-glass windows or skylights to dim the glare.

Govantes and Cabarrocas, perspective of the project for the Juan de Pedro Baró residence, El Vedado, 1927 (above)
Rafael Goyeneche and José Alejo Sánchez, Havana Yacht Club, Playa de Marianao, 1924 (below)

Official architecture, mostly built by renowned local designers and outstanding architects from Europe and the United States, and vernacular architecture, conceived in most cases by contractors, adapted efficiently to the various legislative and city planning parameters regarding the facades, the heights of buildings, the presence or absence of porches, and adjoining walls, among other things. Many architects favored the aesthetic codes imposed by Eclecticism, and applied them to government buildings and residences of the wealthy. Clubs and associations also found in this style a way to show their prominence: both regional Spanish and high bourgeois associations of Havana possess the most impressive facades and lavish indoor decorations of all Cuban architecture. Havana continues to be marked by Eclectic architecture, which is precisely why it stands apart from cities in other Latin American countries where Eclectic architecture disappeared during the construction boom and land speculation of the 1950s, 1960s, and 1970s.

Art Nouveau While at its peak, this style, followed mainly by contractors, was strongly censured by professional architects. Perhaps they believed that its reference to the anti-historic movement in Europe or its use of ornaments made by migrant craftsmen of Catalonian descent contradicted "high art" and the historicist aesthetic codes that leading Cuban architects were trying to impose during the first years of the Republic. The Trade, Agriculture, and Women's Handicraft fair held in 1911 at the Quinta de los Molinos park was a decisive event in the official presentation of this style. The fair included buildings in the Art Nouveau style—highlighting the ornamental value of curved lines—and publicized the various workshops where these decorative elements were manufactured. The Dámaso Gutiérrez residence at La Víbora is one of the best examples of this style, although at present most of Havana's Art Nouveau buildings are in a state of disrepair. Nevertheless, the gracefulness and originality with which the promoters of this trend approached architecture are still evident in all of the buildings' facades, where slender, twisted columns support small domes or balconies with curved asymmetrical openings and polychrome ceramics, and anthropomorphic and zoomorphic figures and plants adorn their wall surfaces. Free and undulating lines, outdoor ironwork, and intricate carpentry link Cuban Art Nouveau to its greatest source of inspiration: Catalonian Modernism.

Mario Rotllant, Pabéllon Mosaicos "La Cubana" ("La Cubana" tiled pavilion) in the Trade, Agriculture, and Women's Handicraft Fair, Havana, 1911

Art Deco In contrast to Art Nouveau, Art Deco was characterized by straight lines, geometrical forms, and stylized decorations in which vertical elements prevailed. Main indoor spaces, such as foyers or spacious rooms, were decorated with bright, polished elements, as those found in the Bacardí, López Serrano, and El País buildings. There are still hundreds of Art Deco structures, most of which are multifamily buildings along important Havanan avenues such as San Lazaro Street in Centro Habana. There are also many examples of private homes such as the Manuel López Chaves house, which stands out among them, not only because it was designed completely in this style, but also because it is well preserved. The abundance of Art Deco examples can be explained by the consolidation of modern ideas from both Europe and the United States at the end of the 1920s, as well as the ease with which builders could rely on workshops to mass produce Art Deco ornamental elements. The Art Deco style continued through the early 1950s, although its peak occurred between 1927 and 1935. By the end of the 1930s, however, the American Streamlined Style began to replace the Art Deco aesthetic with its moderate use of geometrical lines and curved angles, minimal borders, isolated details, and ad hoc manner of defining architectural volumes. Terraces, porches, balconies, and staircases were added to the walls using bitumen textures imitating natural stone. By the end of the 1930s, there were four distinctly different stylistic trends in Havana. Eclecticism was still prevalent especially in the design of private homes; Art Deco remained in vogue (and it is during this period that most apartment buildings were built in this style); Streamlined Style was becoming very popular in government buildings and private homes alike; and Modernism was already gaining attention for its buildings completely devoid of decoration.

Fully modern buildings, with low elevations emphasized by horizontal lines, were in place by the end of the 1940s. Yet **Modernism**

it was not until the 1950s, through a search for Cuba's roots combined with principles of modern architectural design, that an original modern Cuban style emerged. Cuban architects began tailoring international models to the tropical climate, so that certain elements of the International Style were recreated as components of traditional Cuban architecture. An example of this can be seen in the large eaves Richard Neutra placed on the Schulthess residence. At the same time and in keeping with Havana's image as a Caribbean city, a commercial trend toward luxurious buildings with balconies, staircases appearing to move to the beat of rhythmic Cuban music, cast iron railings, transparent glass surfaces, and unadorned facades became popular. This architecture is authentic, refreshing, and pleasant. Other diverse solutions for private houses, apartments, and public buildings permeated every neighborhood and were concentrated in newer planned communities such as Nuevo Vedado, Atabey, and Siboney, where Modern architecture prevailed. Predictably, there was little awareness during this period of the value of traditional cities, and some older buildings were torn down to maximize land use and to make room for high-rises.

After the Revolution in 1959, any ongoing development of Havanan architecture was temporarily interrupted. The con-**The Triumph of the Revolution**

struction—and destruction—boom that happened in other cities throughout the world during the 1960s and 1970s did not occur in Havana. During this period, most of the projects in the city focused on the role of the interior, in order to ensure balanced development throughout the island. Although this situation resulted in the neglect of existing buildings, paradoxically it allowed for their almost complete preservation, simultaneously avoiding the assimilation of Brutalist architecture which was invading other cities at the time. Thousands of buildings of great cultural significance were preserved because of this immobility, imbuing Havana with great historical value on the eve of the twenty-first century. The fact that Cuba was not involved in competitive real estate for forty years helped to preserve its built environment and heritage—both sources of amazement for any visitor to Cuba.

Since the adoption of the Foreign Investment Act in 1995, the situation in Havana has continued to change. The number of applications submitted by foreign companies to build in the city's best neighborhoods is increasing, which suggests that a substantial change in the city's image may occur in a relatively short period of time. This leaves the people now living there with the responsibility of developing the Havana of the new century, without allowing the city to lose the appearance that makes it so unique.

Illustrated List of Photographs

2/3 Mark Anthony Pollack residence (courtyard view on right from 1997, before restoration). 15003 21st St. between 150th and

190th Sts., Cubanacán. Architects: Morales and Co., 1930 (Eclecticism)

1 Julio Alvarez Arcos residence (currently a multifamily house). 451 19th St. at the corner of F St., Vedado, ca. 1915 (Eclecticism)

4 Guillermina Pérez residence. 401 J St. at the corner of 19th St., Vedado. Architect: Arturo Marqués, 1930 (Eclecticism)

5 Cuban Telephone Company. 565 Aguila at the corner of Dragones, Centro Habana. Architects: Morales and Co., 1927 (Eclecticism)

6 Alberto de Armas residence (interior). 318 2nd St. at the corner of 5th St., Miramar. Architect: Jorge Luis Echarte, 1926 (Eclecticism)

7 Multifamily house in Vedado, formerly a private villa (Eclecticism)

9 Juan V. Aguilera residence. 608 5th St. between 6th and 8th Sts., Miramar. Architect: Gregorio Pérez de Gabancho, 1932 (Eclecticism)

8 Housing estate. 309–315 34th St. between 3rd and 5th Sts., Miramar, 1940 (Eclecticism)

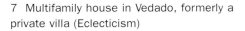

10 Condesa de Buenavista residence (currently a multifamily house). 320 6th St. at the corner of 5th St., Miramar. Architects: Morales and Co., 1928. It received the Rotary Club's "Fachadas Artísticas" award in 1929 (Eclecticism)

11 Villa on Patrocinio between Heredia and José Antonio Saco, Víbora (Eclecticism)

12 Association of the Clerks of Commerce. 207 Prado at the corner of Trocadero, Habana Vieja. Architect: Arturo Amigó; interior decoration: Tomás Mur, 1902–07 (Eclecticism)

13 Residences. 212–214 Paseo between Linea and 11th St., Vedado, ca. 1936 (Eclecticism)

14 Emilio Iglesias residence (currently a multifamily house). 16 O St. between 17th and 19th Sts., Vedado, 1911 (Eclecticism). In the background, the Focsa Building, 55 17th St. between M and N Sts., Vedado. Architect: Ernesto Gómez Sampera, 1950

15 Private residence. 6th St. between 13th and 15th Sts., Vedado (Eclecticism)

16 Cinema Cuba. 309–311 Reina, Centro Habana, 1938 (Eclecticism)

17/18 Row houses on Malecón, Centro Habana (Eclecticism)

19 Palacio de las Ursulinas (far left) and
adjacent structures. 509 Egido between Sol
and Muralla, Habana Vieja. Architect: José
Toraya, 1913 (Eclecticism)

20 El Centro de Oro Building. Reina and
Campanario, Centro Habana. Architect:
Eugenio Dediot, ca. 1910 (Art Nouveau)

21 José Miguel Gómez residence (currently
Casa del Científico), vestibule on the second
level. 212 Prado at the corner of Trocadero,
Habana Vieja. Architect: Hilario del Castillo,
1915 (Eclecticism)

22 Consuelo G. de Riera residence. 117
30th St. between 1st and 3rd Sts., Miramar
1939 (Eclecticism)

23/24 Centro Gallego (currently Gran
Teatro de La Habana), exterior and interior
views. Prado between San Rafael and San

José, Habana Vieja. Architect: Paul Belau,
1915 (Eclecticism)

25 Doorway with Art Nouveau motifs. 267
Mercaderes between Amargura and Teniente
Rey, Habana Vieja

26 Apartment building. 107 Cárdenas
between Gloria and Apodaca, Habana Vieja.
Architect: Mario Rotllant, ca. 1910
(Art Nouveau)

27 Quinta Rosario (currently a secondary
school). 858 Línea between 4th and 6th
Sts., Vedado (Eclecticism)

28 Palacio Cueto (currently a multifamily
house). 351 Inquisidor at the corner of
Mercaderes, Habana Vieja. Architect: Arturo
Marqués, 1905–08 (Art Nouveau)

29 Casa de Dámasco Gutiérrez Cano.
103 Patrocinio between Heredio and José A.
Saco, Diez de Octubre. Architect: Mario
Rotland, ca. 1913 (Art Nouveau)

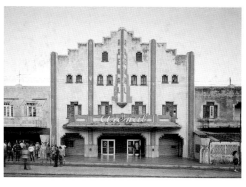

30 Cinema Arenal. 41st St. between 30th
and 34th Sts., Playa (Art Deco)

31 Apartment buildings. 965–967 San
Lázaro between Aramburu and Hospital,
Centro Habana. Architect: Francisco Rexach,
1939/40 (Art Deco)

32 Pilar Antonia Lluch residence. 3438
45th St. between 41st and 34th Sts., Kohly,
Playa, 1941 (Art Deco)

33 Herminia García Bruna residence.
26th St. between 45th and 47th Sts., Kohly,
Playa. Architect: Angel López Valladares,
ca. 1937 (Art Deco)

34/35 Bacardí Building, entrance hall and
exterior view. 261 Monserrate at the corner
of San Juan de Dios, Habana Vieja.

Architects: Esteban Rodríguez Castell,
Rafael Fernández Ruenes, and José
Menéndez Menéndez, 1930 (Art Deco)

36 La Casa Quintana store. 358 Galiano between San Rafael and San Miguel, Centro Habana. Architect: Alejandro Capó Boada, 1937 (Art Deco)

37 Cinema Fausto. 201 Prado at the corner of Colón, Habana Vieja. Architect: Saturnino Parajón, 1938 (Art Deco). It won the Architectural Association's Gold Medal Prize in 1941.

38 López Serrano apartment building. 106 13th St. between L and M Sts., Vedado. Architects: Mira and Rosich, 1931 (Art Deco)

39/40/41 López Serrano Building: window details, entrance hall, and exterior view.

108 13th St. at the corner of L St., Vedado. Architects: Mira and Rosich, 1932 (Art Deco)

42 Apartment building. 478 Galiano at the corner of Zanja, Centro Habana, 1939 (Art Deco)

43 Association of American Writers and Artists (currently Casa de las Américas). G and 3rd Sts., Vedado, 1952 (Art Deco)

44 La Moderna Poesía bookstore. 527 Bernaza at the corner of Obispo, Habana Vieja. Architects: Mira and Rosich, 1938 (Art Deco)

45 Manuel López Chaves residence. 4207 41st St. at the corner of 42nd St., Kohly, Playa. Architect: Esteban Rodríguez Castells, 1932 (Art Deco)

46 Apartment building. 1022 Padre Varela (Belascoain) at the corner of Clavel, Centro Habana (Art Deco)

47 El País Newspaper Building. 158 Reina between San Nicolás and Rayo, Centro Habana. Architects: Cristóbal Díaz and Rafael de Cárdenas, 1941 (Art Deco)

48 Apartment buildings. 964–966 San Lázaro between Aramburu and Hospital, Centro Habana. Architect: Arturo Marqués, 1941, 1940, respectively (Art Deco)

49 Apartment building. 62–64 J St. at the corner of Calzada, Vedado (Art Deco)

50 City residence. 563 Malecón at the corner of Escobar, Centro Habana. Architect: Morales and Co., 1928 (Art Deco)

53 Entrance to the Maca apartment building. 512 12th St. between 21st and 23rd Sts., Vedado. Architect: Luis Delfín Valdés, 1947 (Streamline)

51 Residence. 854–856 25th St. between B and C Sts., Vedado. Architects: Capablanca and Santana, 1949 (Streamline)

52 Ricardo Hernández Beguerie residence. 2808 3rd St. between 28th and 30th Sts., Miramar, 1939 (Streamline)

54 Mercedes L. Navarro residence. 1656 23rd St. between 30th and 32nd Sts., Vedado, 1938 (Streamline)

55/56 Emilio Vasconcelos residence, dining room and exterior view. 1208 21st St.

between 18th and 20th Sts., Vedado. Architect: Emilio Vasconcelos, 1938 (Streamline)

57 Paseo del Prado. Architects: Jean-Claude-Nicolas Forestier and Raúl Otero, 1929

58 Apartment building. 6003–6005 19th St. between 60th and 62nd Sts., Ampliación de Almendares, Playa, 1944 (Streamline)

59 Olan Tower Building. 101 Calzada at the corner of M St., Vedado. Architect: Antonio Santana, 1953 (Modern Movement)

60 Cinema Riviera. 507 23rd St. between G and H Sts., Vedado. The original building (1927) was renovated in 1957 by José Luaces, architect (Modern Movement)

61 Apartment building. 6 L St. between 5th St. and Calzada, Vedado. Architect: Cristóbal Martínez Márquez, 1948/1957 (Modern Movement)

62 Cuban Tobacco Industry Building. Boyeros and 100th St., Boyeros (Modern Movement)

63 Alfred de Schulthess residence. 15012 19th St. between 150th and 190th Sts., Cubanacán. Architects: Richard Neutra and Alvarez & Gutiérrez; landscaping: Robert Burle Marx, 1956. It won the Architectural Association's Gold Medal Prize in 1958 (Modern Movement)

64 House of the Hebrew Community (synagogue). 259 13th St. at the corner of I St., Vedado. Architect: Aquiles Capablanca, 1953 (Modern Movement)

65 School of Dentistry. Salvador Allende and G Sts., Playa. Architect: Esteban Rodríguez Castells, 1942 (Modern Classicism)

66 Offices, currently the Ministry of Justice. O St. between 23rd St. and Humboldt, Vedado. Architect: José Castro Ansa, 1952–54 (Modern Movement)

67 Private residence. 118 28 St. between 1st and 3rd Sts., Miramar, 1947 (Modern Movement)

70 Apartment building. 503 Malecón between Perseverancia and Lealtad, Centro Habana. Architects: Mira and Rosich, 1959 (Modern Movement)

68 Sephardic Hebrew Center of Cuba. 462 17th St. between E and F Sts., Vedado. Architect: Jaime Benavent, 1960 (Modern Movement)

69 Bartolomé Masó Secondary School. Padre Varela (Belascoain) between Concepción de la Valla and Figuras, Centro Habana (Modern Classicism)

71 Apartment building. 312 28th St. between 3rd and 5th Sts., Miramar. Architect: Alberto Prieto, 1953

72 Apartment building. 107–113 Marina, Centro Habana. Architect: Victor M. Morales, 1951 (Modern Movement)

73 Modern "redesign" of an Eclectic building. 357 Reina between Escobar and Lealtad, Centro Habana, ca. 1989.

74 Residential high-rise. 51 Malecón, Centro Habana. Architects: Mira and Rosich, 1958 (Modern Movement)

75 Row houses. Malecón between Galiano and Manrique, Centro Habana (Eclecticism)

76 Solimar Building. 205 Soledad at the corner of San Lázaro, Centro Habana. Architect: Manuel Copado, 1944 (Modern Movement)

77 Apartment Building. Malecón and F St., Vedado. Architect: Antonio Quintana, 1967 (Modern Movement)

78 Private residence (currently a multifamily house). 509–511 Malecón at the corner of Lealtad, Centro Habana. Designer: Alberto de Castro, engineer, 1907 (Eclecticism)